An All-Too-Human Virus

An All-Too-Human Virus

Jean-Luc Nancy

Translated by Cory Stockwell, Sarah Clift
and David Fernbach

polity

Originally published in French as *Un trop humain virus* © Bayard Editions, 2020

This English edition © Polity Press, 2022

Polity Press
65 Bridge Street
Cambridge CB2 1UR, UK

Polity Press
101 Station Landing
Suite 300
Medford, MA 02155, USA

All rights reserved. Except for the quotation of short passages for the purpose of criticism and review, no part of this publication may be reproduced, stored in a retrieval system or transmitted, in any form or by any means, electronic, mechanical, photocopying, recording or otherwise, without the prior permission of the publisher.

ISBN-13: 978-1-5095-5021-0 (hardback)
ISBN-13: 978-1-5095-5022-7 (paperback)

A catalogue record for this book is available from the British Library.

Library of Congress Control Number: 2021939031

Typeset in 12.5 on 15 pt Adobe Garamond by
Cheshire Typesetting Ltd, Cuddington, Cheshire
Printed and bound in Great Britain by CPI Group (UK) Ltd, Croydon

The publisher has used its best endeavours to ensure that the URLs for external websites referred to in this book are correct and active at the time of going to press. However, the publisher has no responsibility for the websites and can make no guarantee that a site will remain live or that the content is or will remain appropriate.

Every effort has been made to trace all copyright holders, but if any have been overlooked the publisher will be pleased to include any necessary credits in any subsequent reprint or edition.

For further information on Polity, visit our website:
politybooks.com

Contents

Publisher's Note   vii
Preface   viii

Prologue   1

1. An All-Too-Human Virus   5

2. 'Communovirus'   13

3. Let Us Be Infants   19

4. Evil and Power   27

5. Freedom   35

6. Neoviralism   40

7. To Free Freedom   45

CONTENTS

8. The Useful and the Useless   58

9. Still All Too Human   68

Appendix 1. Interview with Nicolas Dutent   79

Appendix 2. From the Future to the Time to Come: The Revolution of the Virus, with Jean-François Bouthors   91

Sources of the Texts   102

Publisher's Note

The Preface, Prologue, Chapters 1, 4, and 7 and the Appendices were translated by Cory Stockwell.

Chapters 3, 5, 6, 8, and 9 were translated by Sarah Clift.

Chapter 2 was translated by David Fernbach.

The material included in the Prologue was added to the English edition of this book.

Preface

1. The texts in this volume were assembled at the initiative of Suzanne Doppelt, for the publisher Bayard, in June 2020, at the (very provisional) end of the period of lockdown, and then of progressive opening, in France. The intention was to keep a record of the reactions to the event brought about by the numerous demands and initiatives that arose at the time – at the very least, of the reactions of one of the numerous 'philosophers' (this term took on a very broad meaning) that were expressed at that moment. For me, this concerned in particular the YouTube channel created by Jérôme Lèbre, 'Philosophizing in the Time of the Epidemic', which ended up including about a hundred interventions. There was also

Antinomie, the Italian online journal created by Federico Ferrari and his friends, and many other instances. It was thus very clear that the pandemic, even before it was given its name, brought about a properly viral proliferation of discourse. This was ridiculed, and rightly so. But it is no less right to listen to what was said, for better or for worse (and whether we like it or not), in an urgent situation marked by anxiety and a sudden loss of bearings.

And all the more so as this sudden disarray brought to light an unmooring of certainties or of habits, one that has been active and corrosive for a long time now in the public mind and in the sensibility of developed societies, particularly in Europe. Having emerged from the fault lines or the fissures of what for a long time we took to be western infallibility, the virus was almost immediately perceived as something that revealed – indeed, deconstructed – the fragile and uncertain state of our rational and smoothly functioning civilization.

This is also why it reveals, in a light that is harsher than ever, the exacerbated and unjustifiable gaps between regions, countries, classes and layers of a world that, in becoming more interconnected, is at the same time split asunder, torn apart by its own exponential growth.

Today, a few days after 15 August, in other words less than three months after the end of the lockdown in France, the resumption of the epidemic is already the subject on everyone's lips; elsewhere in the world, above all in the United States and Brazil, it has raged even more than in Europe; just about everywhere, we keep watch, we measure, and we work to halt new developments. At the same time we are beginning to register the grave economic effects of the phenomenon.

The wait for an effective treatment has become so arduous that the head of state of 'great Russia' has judged it appropriate to pre-empt the laboratories by announcing the completion of a vaccine that is still in the test phase. Broadly speaking, heightened anxiety and feverish competition have combined to whet the desire for power. The virus catalyses forms of solidarity but also tensions, judging by the difficulties that Europe's decision in favour of a joint aid package worth €500 billion (the implementation of which must still be overseen) has had to overcome. The telluric movements of global geopolitics are being felt in all their intensity, together with the no less telluric movements of technoeconomic powers.

Tellus, the Roman divinity of earth, also associated with the underworld, holds the powers of life and death.

*

2. The virus is single-handedly revealing a world that for a long time now has been feeling the distress of a profound mutation. What is at stake is not simply the organization of forms of domination: an entire organism feels sick. What is being called into question is an obstinate confidence in the belief in progress and in unpunished predatory behaviour – but without any new conviction arising about the possibility of inhabiting the world humanely.

Not so long ago, these words of Hölderlin used to come up often in learned discourse: 'Poetically man dwells on this earth.' We sought to find virtue in the precious sounds these words made in our throats. We almost always forgot to cite the entire sentence: 'Full of merits, but poetically, man dwells on this earth.'[1] The 'poetic' is, if not

---

1 Tr.: Friedrich Hölderlin, 'In Lovely Blueness . . .', in his

opposed, then at least contraposed to the 'merits' of humans, namely their achievements and their acquisitions. The German word *Verdienst* has, first and foremost, the sense of 'gain, profit'. If, already for Hölderlin, it is in spite of their exploits that humans live or can live in a poetic mode, we must say that, today, it is in spite of their poetic nature or vocation that humans lose themselves in the abundance of their conquests, with all their consequences: destruction, misery and aberrance.

The COVID-19 pandemic is merely the symptom of a more serious illness, which touches humanity in its very ability to breathe, in its capacity to speak and think beyond information and calculation.

It is possible that this symptom will make us see the necessity of combating the pathology beneath it, and will force us to go in search of a vaccine against the success and the domination of self-destruction. It is also possible that other

Poems and Fragments, trans. Michael Hamburger. Ann Arbor: University of Michigan Press, 1968, p. 601; translation slightly modified in accordance with Nancy's text (Hamburger translates *voll Verdienst* with 'full of acquirements').

symptoms will follow this one, up to and including the inflammation and the dying out of vital organs. This would mean that human life, like all life, is reaching its end.

Prologue

Viral Exception

Giorgio Agamben, an old friend, declares that the coronavirus scarcely differs from a normal case of the flu. He forgets that we have a vaccine for the 'normal' flu that has proved its effectiveness. It must still be adapted every year to viral mutations. For all that, the 'normal' flu still kills people – and the coronavirus, for which no vaccine exists, is much more likely to have a lethal outcome: proportionally (according to sources similar to those cited by Agamben), about thirty times more likely. The least one can say is that this is no minor difference.

Giorgio assures us that governments are looking for pretexts to introduce every imaginable state of exception. He does not mention that the exception becomes the rule in a world in which technological interconnections of all kinds (movements, transfers of all kinds, infusions or propagations of substances, etc.) reach a hitherto unknown level of intensity, one that increases along with the population. The growth of the latter in rich countries also involves longer life-spans and an increase in the number of elderly people and, in general, of people at risk.

Make no mistake about the target here: an entire civilization is at stake, there is no doubt about it. There is a sort of viral – biological, computerized, cultural – exception that 'pandemicizes' us. Governments are not the sad agents of this exception, and lashing out at them looks more like an exercise in diversion than real political reflection.

I noted that Giorgio is an old friend. I regret to bring in a personal memory, but in doing so I'm not departing, in essence, from a register of general reflection. Almost thirty years ago, the doctors said that I needed a heart transplant. Giorgio was one of the very few people who advised me not to listen to them. If I had followed his advice, I would undoubtedly have died quite quickly. Everyone makes mistakes. For all that, Giorgio's spirit is no less endowed with a subtlety and a kindness that one can call – without the least bit of irony – exceptional.

February 2020

*

More than a year after our first exchange on the subject of what was not yet termed a 'pandemic' at that point, Giorgio Agamben and I have maintained our respective positions. Today he considers the vaccination to be a futile religion, while I see in it more of a combination of achievement and uncertainty – both technological – that corresponds to the general situation of the civilization from which the pandemic originated. I understand that Giorgio considers our society's obsession with health to be pathetic. Like him, I have Nietzsche's concept of 'great health' in mind. But when an entire civilizational organism is ill – and made all the more so by its obsession with health – it is understandable that it seeks a way out of the illness. Perhaps we will not find a way out, or will not do so unscathed – and this will perhaps present new opportunities. But the already ancient critique of religion, however it might be formulated, has not yet managed to bring about a new civilization.

April 2021

I

An All-Too-Human Virus

As has often been said, Europe exported its wars after 1945. Having destroyed itself, it didn't know what to do other than spread its disunion through its former colonies, in accordance with its alliances and tensions with the world's new poles of power. Between these poles it was no more than a memory, even though it pretended to have a future.

Now Europe imports. Not only merchandise, as it has done for a long time, but first and foremost populations, which is not new either, but is becoming urgent, and indeed overwhelming, at the same rate as exported conflicts and climatic turmoil (which were born in this same Europe). And today it has come to import a viral epidemic.

What does this mean? Not only the fact of a propagation, which has its carriers and its routes. Europe is not the centre of the world, far from it, but it is doing its utmost to play its old role of model or example. There may be strong attractions or impressive opportunities elsewhere: traditional ones, at times a little worn out, as in North America, or newer ones in Asia and in Africa (Latin America is different, having many European characteristics that are mixed with others). But Europe seemed to remain desirable, or more or less believed itself to be so, at least as a refuge.

The old theatre of exemplarities – right of law, science, democracy, appearances and well-being – still gives rise to desires, even if its objects are worn out, indeed out of order. It thus remains open to spectators even if it is not very welcoming to those who don't have the means to fulfil these desires. It shouldn't be surprising if a virus enters the theatre as well.

Nor should it be surprising if it triggers more confusion here than where it was born. Because in China everything has returned to working order, whether we are talking about markets or illnesses. In Europe, by contrast, there has been disorder – between nations and between aspirations. The result was indecision, agitation, and a difficult adaptation. Across the way, the United States immediately rediscovered its superb isolationism and its ability to make clear decisions. Europe has always searched for itself – at the same time as it searched for the world, discovering it, exploring it and exploiting it before once again getting to a point where it no longer knew where it was.

While the first hotbed of the epidemic looks as if it will soon be under control, and while many countries that are still relatively unaffected are closing their borders to Europeans as they had to the Chinese, Europe is becoming the centre of the epidemic. It seems to have brought together the effects of trips to China (business, tourism, study), those of visitors from China and elsewhere (business, tourism, study), those of its general uncertainty, and finally those of its internal disagreements.

It would be tempting to caricature the situation thus: in Europe it's 'Every man for himself!', and elsewhere it's 'It's you and me, virus!'. Or, alternatively, in Europe hesitation, scepticism and the desire to reject received ideas play a larger role than in many other regions. This is the heritage of libertine, libertarian and reasoning reason – in other words of what for us, old Europeans, represented the very life of the mind.

It is thus that the inevitable repetition of the expression 'emergency measures' causes the ghost of Carl Schmitt to emerge, through a sort of hasty conflation. The virus thus propagates discourses of ostentatious bravado. Not being fooled becomes more important than avoiding contagion – which amounts to being doubly fooled – and perhaps fooled by a poorly repressed anxiety. Or by a puerile sentiment of impunity or bravado . . .

Everyone (myself included) chips in with a critical, doubting or interpretative remark. Philosophy, psychoanalysis and political commentary about the virus are all the rage.

(Let's exempt from this schema the delicious poem by Michel Deguy, 'Coronation', on the website of the journal *Po&sie*.)

Everyone is discussing and arguing, because we have long been accustomed to difficulty, ignorance and undecidability. On a global scale it seems, by contrast, that assurance, control and decision are dominant. This, at least, is the image that we might make for ourselves, or that tends to be composed in the global imaginary.

The coronavirus, as a pandemic, is indeed in every way a product of globalization. It is a precise expression of the latter's traits and tendencies; it is an active, pugnacious and effective free-trade advocate. It takes part in the broad process by which cultures come undone; what it affirms is not so much a culture as a mechanics of forces that are inextricably technical, economic, dominating and, if need be, physiological or physical (think of petroleum, of the atom). It is true that at the same time the model of growth is called into question, such that the French head of state feels compelled to make mention of it. It is quite possible that we will indeed be forced to shift our algorithms – but nothing indicates that this might give rise to another way of thinking.

Because it is not enough to eradicate a virus. If technical and political mastery turns out to be its own end, it will make of the world a simple field of forces that are ever more strained against one another, stripped of all the civilizing pretexts that were effective in the past. The contagious brutality of the virus grows into a brutality of management. We are already faced with the need to choose between those who are and those who are not eligible for care. (We have not yet said anything about the economic and social injustice that is sure to ensue.) We are not dealing here with the devious calculations of some Machiavellian conspirators. There are no particular abuses by states. There is only the general law of interconnections, control over which is what is at stake for technoeconomic powers.

*

The pandemics of the past could be seen as divine punishments, just as sickness in general was for a long time exogenous to the social body. Today the majority of sicknesses are endogenous, produced by our living conditions, food supply and ingestion of toxic substances. What was divine has become human – all too human, as Nietzsche says. Modernity was for a long time best expressed by Pascal's words: 'man infinitely surpasses man'.[1] But if humans surpass themselves 'too much' – that is, without elevating themselves any longer to Pascal's divine – then

1 Tr.: Blaise Pascal, *Pensées*, trans. A. J. Krailsheimer. London: Penguin, 1995, p. 35 (7.434); translation slightly modified.

they no longer surpass themselves at all. Instead, they get bogged down in a humanity that is surpassed by the events and the situations it has produced.

The virus attests to the absence of the divine, because we know its biological constitution. We are even discovering to what point the living being is more complex and less comprehensible than our previous representations of it led us to think, and to what extent the exercise of political power – that of a people, that of a supposed 'community', for example 'European', or that of strongman regimes – is another form of complexity, one that is also less comprehensible than it seems. We understand better the extent to which the term 'biopolitics' is ridiculous under these conditions: life and politics both defy us. Our scientific knowledge invites us to be dependent solely on our own technical power, but there is no pure and simple technicity, because knowledge itself brings with it uncertainty (it's enough to read the studies that are being published). Technical power is not unequivocal; so how can a political power that is expected to respond at the same time to objective data and to legitimate expectations be any less equivocal?

Of course, we must presume that objectivity will guide our decisions. If this objectivity is one of 'lockdown' or 'distancing', how far should the authorities go to ensure that it is respected? And of course, from the opposite standpoint, whence arises the self-interested arbitrariness of a government that seeks to preserve the Olympic Games (this is just one example among many), from which it, and many of the businesses and managers for whom it is partly an instrument, expect to benefit? Or the self-interested arbitrariness of a government that seizes the occasion to stir up nationalism?

The magnifying glass of the virus enlarges the features of our contradictions and our limits. It is a reality principle that knocks at the door of our pleasure principle. Death accompanies it. The death that we exported through wars, famines and devastations, that we believed to be confined to a few other viruses and to the various forms of cancer (themselves in a quasi-viral expansion), is lying in wait for us at the nearest street corner. Just think! We are humans, bipeds without feathers endowed with language, but surely neither superhuman nor transhuman. All too human? Must we not rather understand that we never can be?

2

'Communovirus'

An Indian friend of mine tells me that back home they talk about the 'communovirus'. How could we not have thought of that already? It's so obvious! And what an admirable and complete ambivalence: a virus coming from communism, a virus that communizes us. That is much more fertile than the derisory 'corona', which evokes old monarchical or imperial histories. And 'communo-' is good for dethroning 'corona', if not decapitating it.

This is what it seems to be doing in its first meaning, since the virus comes from the largest country in the world, whose regime is officially communist. It is not just officially so: as President Xi Jinping has said, its management of the viral

epidemic demonstrates the superiority of a social-
ist system with Chinese characteristics. Although
communism consists essentially in the abolition of private property, Chinese communism
has consisted, for many years now, in a careful
combination of collective (or state) property and
private property (apart from land ownership).[1]

As we know, this combination has led to
remarkable growth in China's economic and
technical capacities and in its global role. It is
still too soon to know how to designate the society produced by this combination: in what sense
is it communist and in what sense has it intro-
duced the virus of individual competition, even
in its ultraliberal extreme? For the time being,
COVID-19 has enabled China to demonstrate
the effectiveness of the collective and statal aspect
of its system. This effectiveness has proved itself
to the point that China is now coming to the aid
of Italy and France.

Of course, there is no shortage of commentary
on the enhanced authoritarian power that the
Chinese state is currently enjoying. In fact it is

1 Tr.: Here the published text has 'individual property',
which seems accidental in view of the author's use of the term
in what follows.

just as if the virus appeared at the right time to shore up official communism. What is irksome is that in this way the meaning of the word 'communism' gets ever more blurred – and it was already uncertain.

Marx wrote very precisely that private property had meant the disappearance of collective property, and that both would be replaced in due course by what he called 'individual property'. By this he did not mean goods owned individually (i.e. private property), but the possibility for individuals to become properly themselves, to realize themselves, one could say. Marx did not have the time or the means to take this line of thought further. But we can at least recognize that it already opens up a convincing – if very indeterminate – perspective on a 'communist' proposal. 'To realize oneself' does not mean acquiring material or symbolic goods; it means becoming real, effective, existing in a unique way.

We need, then, to dwell on the second meaning of 'communovirus'. In fact the virus does communize us. It essentially puts us on a basis of equality, bringing us together in the need to make a common stand. That this has to involve the isolation of each of us is simply a paradoxical way of experiencing our community. We can be unique only together. This is what makes for our most intimate community: the shared sense of our uniquenesses.

Today we are reminded in every way of our togetherness, interdependence and solidarity. Testimonies and initiatives of this sort are coming from all sides. If we add to this the decline in air pollution that is due to the reduction of transport and industry, some people already anticipate with delight the overthrow of technocapitalism. We should not scoff at this fragile euphoria, but rather ask ourselves how far we can better understand the nature of our community.

Solidarity is called for and activated on a large scale, but the overall media landscape is dominated by the expectation of state welfare – which Emmanuel Macron took the opportunity to celebrate. Instead of confining ourselves, we feel confined primarily by force, even if for the sake of our own welfare. We experience isolation as a deprivation, even when it is a protection.

In a way, this is an excellent catch-up session: it is true that we are not solitary animals. It is true that we need to meet up, have a drink and visit. Besides, the sudden rise in phone calls, emails and other social flows shows a pressing need, a fear of losing contact.

Does this mean that we are in a better position to reflect on this community? The problem is that the virus is still its main representative; that, between the surveillance model and the welfare model, only the virus remains as a common property.

If this is the case, we will make no progress in understanding what transcending both collective and private property could mean – that is, transcending both property in general and what it designates in terms of the possession of an object by a subject. The characteristic of the 'individual', to speak as Marx did, is to be incomparable, incommensurable and unassimilable – even to him- or herself. It is not to possess 'goods'. It is for each individual to be a unique, exclusive possibility of realization, whose exclusive uniqueness is realized, by definition, only between all and with all – also against all or in spite of all, but always in relation and exchange (communication). This is a 'value' that is neither one of the general equivalent (money), nor therefore one of an extorted 'surplus value' – but a value that cannot be measured in any way.

Are we capable of thinking in such a difficult and even dizzying way? It is good that the
'communovirus' forces us to ask ourselves this
question. For it is only on this condition that
it is worth, in the end, working to eliminate it.
Otherwise we will end up back at the starting
point. We will be relieved, but should be prepared for other pandemics.

3

Let Us Be Infants

It is difficult to speak when speech reveals its own impoverishment. All speech today, whether technoscientific, political, philosophical or moral, is showing its weakness. There is no guaranteed knowledge, no available programme of action or thought. There is no affirmation of solidarity that can measure up to the need to maintain distance, no affirmation of universality that need not take into account glaring local disparities. There is no vision of the world because there is no visible world, and there is also no perspective on the future since we don't know how the pandemic might evolve. We are doubtless sure of only one thing: of the enormous ecological or 'econological' difficulties that await us regardless of the outcome of the pandemic. And the fact that this very pandemic is suddenly cleaning the air of regions in lockdown does not mean that we know better than before how industry and technology can be reorganized.

Moreover, speech is being impoverished by pain and sadness, by the aching awareness of the threat and the deaths that are adding to the already overwhelming cruelty of famines, persecutions, all the other epidemics, endemic illnesses and terrible conditions of life.

Of course, we often hear it said that an entire system is showing its fault lines – but that in itself is nothing new. It can be written on walls, as Gérard Bensussan saw it in Strasbourg – 'The virus is capitalism' – and we can speak of the 'capitalovirus', just as we spoke of the 'communovirus' (which is basically the same thing). As if we had found new energy to denounce the old enemy that seemed to have triumphed . . . As if, above all, by saying the word 'capitalism' we had exorcised the devil by at least half.

But in doing that we forget that this devil is indeed very old and that it supplied the motor for the entire history of the modern world. It has existed for at least seven centuries, if not more. Throughout that time, the unlimited production of market value has become the motor of society and also, in a sense, its *raison d'être*. The effects were spectacular: a new world emerged. It could be that this world and its *raison d'être* are in the process of breaking down, but without giving us anything with which to replace them. We might even be tempted to say: on the contrary.

Let us judge the progress we have made. In 1865, one M. Gaudin, who presented himself as a 'chemist-philosopher', was able to claim that, if one accepted common belief, people of his time were witness to the emergence of many diseases that had been unknown to their ancestors. Yet these diseases, formally localized, very probably spread as a result of the network of rapid communications between very distant countries that already existed in Gaudin's day. So, for almost two centuries, our own progress will have confirmed and reinforced this hypothesis, while failing to confirm the remedy proposed by the same chemist-philosopher (the remedy was based on the administration of ozone).

This progress has given us the aeroplane, the rocket, the refrigerator, Bakelite, penicillin and cybernetics. At the same time, it has placed the entire world within a regime of market value and of substantial widening of the gap between a wealth that increases on its own and the poverty that this growth produces as its spin-off or waste. However, in this same progress, society has also stripped itself of everything that made it possible to produce social hierarchies, to legitimize the power of some over others or to justify punishments or rewards by means of natural or supernatural justice. Human beings became equal before the law and inequalities became intolerable at exactly the same pace at which they were intensified.

The virus that follows the routes and rhythms of the global circulation of goods (of which humans are a part) spreads through a contagion that is more effective than that of rights. In a sense it equalizes existences: it killed Manu Dibango as well as Marguerite Derrida, José Luis Capón or Julie A.[1] It thus recalls the sovereign right that

1 Respectively a Cameroonian musician, Jacques Derrida's spouse, a Spanish former soccer player, and a French high school student.

death exercises over life, because it is part of life. It is no doubt this right that in the end justifies the right of everyone to the same existence.

Indeed, perhaps being mortal makes us equal when there are no longer any supernatural or natural differences. There is a good chance that the pandemic will shed new light on the inequalities of today's world. For, even if the virus does not carry out a kind of 'social sorting', the fact remains that some conditions of life are more favourable than others to being protected against the contagion. Up until now, this has mostly been a concern for urban populations, especially their social strata most likely to travel, whether for business, for study or for holidays. And they are also the ones who can best self-isolate at home – to say nothing of their second homes. But when it comes to the living conditions in Gaza or in the Brazilian favelas, or to those of a large segment of the Indian population – to limit ourselves to these examples – we can fear the worst. Likewise, in the suburbs of large European cities, the phenomenon is already noticeable, as it is on the Turkish–Greek border. The virus 'arrives by plane with the rich but will explode among the poor', as one Brazilian official put it.

Everything can be summed up in this one question: when water is scarce, how are you supposed to engage in frequent handwashing?

That is not all. Economic activity is affected at every level, but there are huge differences between multinational business, the independent businessperson and the shoeshiner on the street. The idea of a so-called 'universal' basic income has been coming back for some time now, as a way of responding to the virus's morbid egalitarianism. But, regardless of what technical measures are taken, they will have to be such as to challenge the truly obscene income gap that we have seen for far too long. And this applies not only to the period of the pandemic – the duration of which cannot, in any case, be predicted. It will also have to apply to any recovery, remediation, reconstruction or innovation that will follow, as long as there is a follow-up.

All of this we know. I am just repeating what fills newspapers, radios, televisions and networks, every day and every night. But, more often than not, we hear talk about what it's going to take or announcements about what is to come. We believe we can anticipate. Anticipation is necessary, but always necessarily limited and fragile.

What matters is the present: it is now, in the midst of fear and sadness, that we are asking ourselves whether we know what we want, whether we have understood that the very principle of our civilization – let's call it technocapitalist – is being called into question. We have understood, or we should have understood, that equality is not some agreeable utopia but an existential requirement – that market equivalence culminates in delusional cruelty and in what Marx, citing Lucretius, called the *mors immortalis* ['deathless death'] of capital – and that therefore the word 'communism' really conveys the deep meaning of a resistance to our self-destruction, even if that meaning still hasn't been achieved.

Marx said that this world lacks spirit: for us, this word has become suspect or stupid. But it only designates breath, or what brings life: precisely what the coronavirus impairs. We have a lot of ideas, a lot of notions, a lot of knowledge and a lot of representations. But spirit has run out of breath amid all those computations.

We must relearn how to breathe and to live, quite simply. Which is a lot, and difficult, and long – children [*les enfants*] know this. The *infantes* ['those without words or speech', 'the mute':

Latin plural of *infans*, 'babe'], they don't know how to speak. They don't know how to modulate their breath in speech. But they only ask to learn, and they learn and then they speak. Let us be infants. Let us re-create a language. Let us have this courage.

4

Evil and Power*

The pandemic is something bad – this is a point on which there is little discussion. Certainly, there are a few voices that declare that it's not all that bad. They point out that already existing illnesses and the wars that are still under way cause many more deaths. This is a strange argument, because

* Tr.: The original title, 'Le mal et la puissance', requires an explanatory note. The most common translation of the noun *mal* is 'evil', though it can also mean 'wrong', 'bad', 'damage', 'harm', or even 'ache', depending on the context. As an adverb, however, *mal* means 'badly' or 'poorly', and Nancy employs the term both as adverb and as noun throughout. There is a further complication. In the essay's sixth paragraph, Nancy divides evil into three categories: illness, misfortune and wrongdoing. In French, these terms are all compounds of *mal-*: *maladie*, *malheur* and *malfaisance*. The reader should keep this lexical richness in mind while reading the essay.

27

it in no way diminishes the addition of a supplementary deadliness, one that, up to this point, could not be controlled without a considerable and costly (in every sense of these terms) mobilization. Others maintain that the real evil is to be found in the voluntary servitude of a society that is concerned only with its well-being and that triggers a dangerous governmental and medical coddling – as though it were necessary to invent an abstract heroism, one lacking both a cause and a tragic dimension.

Of course, nobody denies that serious societal – indeed, civilizational – questions have been raised, or rather underlined, by the virus. On the contrary, we talk about this endlessly. But, as Descartes would say, the important thing is to speak about it in a pertinent way.

It is most often the word 'capitalism' that is at the forefront of our discussions. To be sure, one cannot deny the responsibility of a system of production and profit that promotes a continuous expansion of economic, technical, cultural and existential dependencies, indeed servitudes. The problem is that, as we said before, it most often seems to suffice to pronounce the word 'capitalism' to have exorcised the demon – after which the good God, whose name is 'ecology', reappears.

We have to say it once more: this demon who supplied the motor for the history of the modern world, configuring and modelling this world, is very old. The unlimited production of market value has become value in itself, society's *raison d'être*. The effects have been spectacular: a new world has emerged. It is possible that this world is in the process of decomposing, but without providing us with anything to replace it. One is even tempted to say 'quite the contrary' when one sees savage practices such as the profiteering by one nation on the masks of another, the flight of a king who goes into lockdown 9,000 kilometres away from his kingdom, the news of a cult whose aim is to provide divine immunization against the virus, or simply the hysterical tussles that form around the presumption of a treatment.

In truth, what is at stake is not only this or that operational defect. It is something that is going badly in a constitutive manner, something inherent in the course the world has taken, or that we have caused it to take, for a long time. And what is going badly is well and truly, if I can put it this way, of the order of the bad or evil. The virus is not evil in itself. But the virulence of the crisis, its immediate and, what is more, foreseeable effect of worsening the conditions of the poorest, allow us to say that it gathers together, in a striking way, the features of evil.

There are three forms of evil: illness, misfortune and wrongdoing [*la maladie, le malheur et la malfaisance*]. Illness is part of life. Misfortune is what causes existence (that is, life that reflects upon itself) to suffer, whether through an illness or an assault (be it natural, social, technological or moral). Wrongdoing (which one could also call cursing [*le maléfice*]) is the deliberate production of an assault or an illness: it targets the being or the person, however one wants to put it.

To what point is contemporary virulence deliberate? To the point where its power is linked or correlated to the complex of its contributing factors or its agents. There is no need to repeat what has been broadly documented and commented upon concerning the development of viral forms and the conditions of contagion offered by contemporary communications, by sites of collaborative research opened at least twenty years ago and by all technological, economic and political interactions.

Analogous complexes bring about pollution, the destruction of species, pesticide poisonings, deforestation, and nothing less than a substantial share of famines, forced migrations, onerous living conditions, impoverishments, unemployment, and other forms of social and moral decomposition. And it is also technoeconomic growth that led to the development of industrial empires on the one hand and, on the other, of totalitarian domination, from its most crushing to its most insidious forms – that is, from camps of all sorts to all manner of exploitations and, finally, to the exhaustion of everything we once called 'politics'.

It is not by chance that the health crisis today comes about after more than a century of accumulated disasters. This crisis is a particularly expressive figure – though less fierce or cruel than many others – of the reversal of our history. Progress has revealed a capacity for wrongdoing long suspected and now recognized. The warnings of Freud, Heidegger, Günther Anders, Jacques Ellul and many others went unheeded, just like all the work that was done to deconstruct the self-sufficiency of the subject, of the will, of humanism. But today it must be acknowledged that humans are undertaking a decidedly human evil, and we should not be surprised if a philosopher, Mehdi Belhaj Kacem, writes: 'Evil is the *primary fact.*'[1]

Evil, for our tradition, has always been a flaw that could be rectified or offset with the aid of God or Reason. It was regarded as a negativity destined to be suppressed or overcome. But it is the Good of our conquest of the world that has turned out to be destructive – and, as such, clearly self-destructive. Abundance destroys abundance; speed kills speed; health damages health; wealth itself is perhaps, in the end, in the process of ruining itself (without any of it going to the poor).

How have we got here? There was undoubtedly a moment starting from which what had been the conquest of the world – of territories, of resources, of forces – turned into the creation of a new world: not only in the sense this expression had once, when it referred to America, but in the sense that the world has literally become the creation of our technoscience, which would therefore be its god. This is called omnipotence. Since

1 Tr.: See Mehdi Belhaj Kacem, 'Le Système du pléonectique: Le mal'. *Mediapart*, 4 December 2019, https://blogs.mediapart.fr/edition/dossier-david-graeber/article/041219/le-systeme-du-pleonectique-le-mal-par-mehdi-belhaj-kacem. My translation.

Averroes, philosophy has known the paradoxes of omnipotence and psychoanalysis has known its hallucinatory deadlock. What is in question is always the possibility or impossibility of limiting such a power.

What might indicate a limit? Perhaps precisely the manifestness of death, of which the virus reminds us: a death that no cause, no war, no power can justify – and that underlines the inanity of so many deaths due to hunger, exhaustion and the barbarity of war, of concentration camps and of doctrines. Knowing that we are mortal not by accident, but by the play of life, and of the life of the mind as well.

If each existence is unique, it is because it is born and it dies. It is because it plays out in this interval that it is unique. David Grossman wrote very recently, concerning the pandemic: 'Just as love causes us to set apart one person from the masses that flow through our life, so, we see now, the awareness of death also causes us to do.'[2]

2 Tr.: See David Grossman, 'The plague is a formative event: When it fades, new possibilities will emerge'. *Haaretz*, 24 March, 2020, https://www.haaretz.com/world-news/.premium.MAGA ZINE-the-plague-is-a-formative-event-when-it-fades-new-possi bilities-will-emerge-1.8687842.

If evil is manifestly linked, in its effects, to the dizzying inequalities of conditions, perhaps nothing gives forth a clearer foundation for equality than mortality. We are not equal by virtue of an abstract law, but rather by virtue of a concrete condition of existence. Knowing ourselves to be finite – positively, absolutely, infinitely and singularly finite – and not indefinitely powerful: this is the only way to give a sense to our existences.

5

Freedom

A young woman was taken into custody for hanging a banner on her balcony that said 'Macronavirus – will it be over soon?' The word 'Macronavirus' had already been circulating for a while and it was hard to see why such a banner would warrant a police operation. Not only is such an operation grotesque, but it is also political policing of the cheapest kind. And we don't need to look very far to discern the motivations of the person whom the police arrested. Even taking into account the extreme difficulty of managing the situation, it is easy to get fed up with the delays, the waffling and the evasions that really take up too much room on the public stage. We could have expected fewer misfires, failures and shortages, less wavering. But in any case this banner did not break any laws and it is unacceptable that one should be invented.

That is why I took part in a protest initiated by a Toulouse collective. There was nothing even remotely despotic or arbitrary about it: I would hope that those who initiated this pitiable operation will be put in their place.

This is all the more necessary as we are already hearing the eager voices of those quick to denounce the loss of our freedoms during lockdown. It really is a bad idea to fuel these discourses – and this for two reasons.

One is technical. Those angered by the lockdown point to strategies involving herd immunity, about which there can be no guarantees whatsoever – as is the case with so many biological and medical aspects of this pandemic. At the same time, they would have preferred to let die those who were going to die soon anyway. Between these two extremes, it is unclear what would happen to those who were experiencing serious respiratory problems but were not necessarily at risk of an imminent death. In general, these ways of seeing are governed by a principle of natural regulation that we must learn to accept. Demands made in order to protect health are viewed as a form of modern voluntary servitude that opens onto new forms of tyranny.

This neoliberal thinking risks encountering problems similar to those of economic liberalism. The two are obviously related. In the same way in which there is a market for goods, there is also one for life, sickness, ageing and death. Let free competition reign unfettered.

It is true that health has tended to become a consumer good and that longevity is becoming a value in itself. This often comes down to accepting styles and qualities of life wherein maintaining life takes precedence over carelessness, or even over the risk-taking that is a normal part of active lives. While that is true, it doesn't mean that we answer it by exposing everyone to each and every risk posed by expanding technoeconomic systems that multiply toxicities, poisonings, auto-immunities, erosions and viralities of all kinds.

That is why the current crisis is not simply a health crisis but is a product of intensified conquests in which we are once again ensnared and bogged down to the point that in fact we no longer know how to get out of them.

On that account, all the whining about restrictions on freedom seems pitiful, especially considering that our ordinary freedoms – those of movement and self-expression – are exercised only within the ever-narrowing framework of our ecotechnical, demographic and ideological needs. This framework is so narrow because, all around, it is necessary to compensate, redress and treat, at the same time as there doesn't seem to be any more history opening up – either for those who only know how to get rich or for those who are forced to become impoverished. For that, finally, is what we have been reduced to.

We are perhaps finally prepared to realize that we are not yet free of the petty freedom of the subject, sure of ourselves and our rights – which are reduced to the right to obey the market of some and the whims of others. We must invent everything anew – including the very meaning of our rights, our humanity, and a 'freedom'.

No philosophy has ever thought of freedom in terms of the simple autonomy of the individual and in complete disregard for its existence in some world – even this world infinitely open beyond itself. Marx said that the world of his own time was 'without spirit'. We are henceforth not only without spirit but perhaps even without any other body than our 'machinic', energetic, cathodic and plasmatic connections. Today's virus and the means of eliminating it – medical, economic and political – are no big deal compared to what awaits us, so long as we have a future.

6

Neoviralism

We have been hearing a lot lately from those who are becoming increasingly vocal in their denunciation of the lockdown. They argue that, by letting the virus and the available immunities run their course, we will achieve – and at a much lower economic cost – a much better result. The human costs would amount only to a slight acceleration of the deaths that were already foreseeable before the pandemic.

The ideologues of what we might christen 'neoviralism' – since it reinscribes economic and social neoliberalism at the level of health – avail themselves of a battery of figures and references that are refuted by those at the forefront of information and research. But this debate does not

interest the neoviralists, who are already con-
vinced of the ignorance, indeed the blindness of
those situated on the front lines of care. And
they don't shy away – if they are ever shy – from
speaking of the subjugation of knowledge to
power, a power itself reputed to be ignorant or
Machiavellian. As for the rest of us, to them we
are suckers.

It is always interesting to watch the givers of lessons emerge. In general, they always arrive a little
late and they repeat history. Indeed, they already
know everything in advance. For instance, that
the conditions of life in long-term care are often
unappealing. Since they knew it already, why did
they not use their knowledge earlier, to improve
the state of things? The question of living conditions, and even of the meaning of lives extended,
at times, mostly by means of medical and social
interventions has been posed for a long time. I
have already heard older people pose it. I have
also heard them ask why they are not allowed to
die sooner.

That said, every person over the age of seventy,
even if suffering from one condition or another,
is not necessarily as good as dead. Assuming a
free trade with the virus, it is the virus that would

have done the sorting in any case – to say nothing of those under seventy, since there are still a few of them around. This logic would make sense if we did not have some means of protection at our disposal. Our systems of medical technoscience are caught in a vicious circle: the more we know how to cure, the more complex and unruly ailments become and the less we can just let nature – which, we know all too well, finds itself in a generally poor state – take its course.

But it is indeed about nature that the neoviralists speak, without saying it: a judicious propensity of nature makes it possible to eliminate viruses by eliminating the useless and miserable elderly. For a while, they were even telling us that this process of elimination might well strengthen the species. And that is what is so intellectually unscrupulous and politically and morally dubious. For, if the issue has to do with our technosciences and their socioeconomic conditions of practice, then the problem lies elsewhere. It is in the very conception of society, its ends and its stakes.

Likewise, when these neoviralists denounce a society that is incapable of accepting death, they forget that all the propensities – both natural and supernatural – that at one time allowed for strong and, in sum, living relationships with death have vanished. Technoscience has broken down the natural and the supernatural. We have not become weaklings: on the contrary, we imagined ourselves to have become all-powerful . . .

*

All the crises in which we are caught – and of which the COVID-19 pandemic is only one minor effect, in comparison to many others – proceed from the unlimited extension of the free use of all the available forces, natural and human, in view of a production that has no end other than itself and its own power. The virus has come at the right time to tell us that there are limits. But the neoviralists are too deaf to hear it: they only hear the noise of the motors and the sizzle of networks. They are also arrogant, full of self-importance and incapable in the slightest of the simple modesty that might arise when reality shows itself to be complex and difficult.

Essentially, even if they are not armed, they act just like those who, elsewhere, demonstrate against the lockdown by carrying assault rifles and grenades. The virus must be convulsing in laughter. But there is rather something to cry about, because neoviralism begins in resentment and leads back to resentment. It wants to avenge itself on the timid beginnings of solidarity and community that are manifesting themselves in new ways. It wants to nip in the bud every inclination to change this self-infected world. It wants nothing to jeopardize free enterprise and free trade, including with viruses. It wants everything to keep turning in circles and sink into the nihilism and barbarity that its so-called freedoms do such a bad job of hiding.

7

To Free Freedom

The lockdown requirements necessitated by the viral pandemic have given rise to numerous protests in the geopolitical and ideological regions that demand the rights we call human. Certainly the most widespread reaction to these requirements has been acceptance and even adoption, but often against a background of regret for what has seemed an infringement of freedoms as much as a measure of health protection.

The more or less hypothetical model of herd immunity has been invoked as a solution that would have allowed us to avoid limiting freedom of movement and gathering. The bans on visiting the sick and the dying were viewed as particularly serious curbs on freedom. We fear that the possibility of tracing the infected is an open invitation to the unlimited monitoring of private life. The announcement of the reopening of schools immediately encountered opposition based on the freedom of self-protection; here the motives are ostensibly reversed, but the underlying principle remains the same: the freedom of every person in every circumstance.

Our society considers its most precious good – so long as health and life are not seriously threatened – to be individual freedom. This can be essentially reduced to the freedom of movement, of gathering, and of expression, as well as to the freedom to weigh in on and take part in the management of our common existence, within legislative frameworks that are themselves freely accepted.

These gains of the modern world are not debatable. One of the essential characteristics of this world is to have eliminated all forms of authority that are not freely consented to, from the right to enslave to the divine or dynastic right to exercise power.

The exercise of this freedom is nonetheless not simple, since, as I just noted, it can demand restrictions as well as oppose them. But the important thing, as we understand very well, is that in every case it should be the free individual who decides. This freedom must coexist with the freedom of others, and must come to terms with common interests and forms of solidarity. But each individual must still be in a position to give assent or refuse it, if only by agreeing to wait for the right moment to change the law.

In every way and on all fronts, every individual who is of age must be able to exercise free judgment (except in cases of legal or medical incapacity, which must itself be established through careful monitoring, itself liable to be called into question). Nothing is more obvious to us than our full freedom of judgment and the freedom to make decisions that flows from it.

This freedom demands to be guaranteed and protected. This is why the only form of social and political organization that suits it is democracy, which consists in the free participation of all in the decisions by which common existence is assured. The community thus formed amounts to the coexistence of free individuals.

The freedom of subjects thus determines the reign, both individual and collective, of this very freedom. This nicely meets the requirements of the only possible definition of freedom – the capacity to act solely according to one's own decision.

One's own or proper decision [*la décision propre*] assumes that the subject is constituted precisely by full self-possession [*par une entière propriété de lui-même*] (and secondarily by what belongs to that subject). What the term 'freedom' contains, for us, is not only of the order of material and social independence (as was the case for our ancestors). It is what is proper to a subject, its capacity for self-determination.[1] In one sense, one might say that freedom and subjectivity are reciprocal and substitutable concepts. As for the equality of subjects, it is determined by the fact that all subjects are identically and thus equally free. Everything that goes beyond this fundamental double postulation – like solidarity or fraternity, as well as inevitable relations of power – is secondary and inferior in ontological dignity.

1 Tr.: The original here is *sa capacité à s'auto-déterminer*. Nancy employs many words in this essay that begin with the prefix *auto-*, which I have generally translated as 'self-' (as in the examples, below, of 'self-determination', 'self-limitation' and 'self-expropriation'), except in cases where words beginning with 'auto-' are clearly the correct choice, such as 'autonomy' and 'automatic'.

We know all this perfectly: these are the axioms of the socio-political, ethical and, in sum, also metaphysical logic of our world. Metaphysics in fact designates the thinking of principles and of ends. Now no representation of principles and ends – be it of the order of a religious law or of any sort of destiny – can satisfy the axioms that I just recalled. The only principle is freedom. This means that freedom also bears the ultimate finality. We are free to be free. Self-founded, freedom is its own end [*Autofondée la liberté est autofinale*].

All the rest, if one thinks about it, is merely subordinate. Productions, possessions, actions and works are in truth merely the marginal side effects of self-affirming freedom.

(I am not unaware that many will not be satisfied by this outline – that they nurture in a more or less fervent way religious, aesthetic or symbolic convictions that offer a meaning of existence not limited to the self-finalizing of one's own freedom. These beliefs fall within the domain of perfectly understandable affective expectations. But either their convictions completely replace freedom – which brings about a conflict – or more or less coherent arrangements allow those who hold these beliefs to live in a double regime, as subject of law on the one hand, faithfully obedient on the other.)

Nevertheless, it must be admitted that the pure apparatus of freedom such as I have just set it out is not without its difficulties. I have in mind not only all the secondary aspects that I evoked, all the practical or affective contingencies that complicate and even obscure the free exercise of freedom.

I have in mind two considerations of a fundamental nature.

The first concerns the history of freedom in the modern world. The second concerns the ontological content itself of our idea of freedom.

Let us begin with the history. It is remarkable, indeed amazing that the modern conquest of freedom – which led from the humanism of the sixteenth century to the democracy of the twentieth – was accompanied by the most severe questioning of this freedom.

It did not take long for the critique of the freedoms declared by humanism and democracy to begin. Very quickly, it was understood that inequalities of property brought about an unequal use of freedom and that this unequal use degraded freedom itself. The simplest and most indispensable of freedoms, that of procuring one's own subsistence, appeared comical when some were free to sell themselves on a labour market and others free to regulate, in sovereign or tyrannical ways, the conditions of this market. All the workers' struggles of the nineteenth and the twentieth centuries were guided by the demand to give a real and non-formal content to the right to work, itself the condition of the exercise of all other rights.

But we have forgotten all that. In fact, that which should have produced, through work, a society whose common freedom would have been – qua communism – the achievement of all, produced only another form of dependence. Conditions of work everywhere became ever more complex and more dependent on techno-economic logics, such that the gap between the freedom of decision makers and the submission of those who executed their decisions only widened. The latter group makes up the vast majority of the population – which also includes an important share of people deprived of work, and thus of freedom.

By contrast, large spaces of freedom opened up in the form of increased choices of consumer goods. To the means of subsistence and comfort were added leisure activities, cultural goods, and what has been described as the passive, indeed addictive absorption of the great spectacle of this overabundance and of our own dependence on it. Freedom has become the recommended use of the images of our capacities for mastery and satisfaction. A large part of the most widespread form of cinema peddles only this content. Everywhere, in other words, the representation of self-determination takes the place of real self-determination.

In fact we have begun to be aware of this enormous illusion of modernity, the illusion of the liberation of a humanity that has overcome all forms of dependence. This awareness is revealed by many signs, and in particular this one: we now know how much of our freedom to act we lose in the profound destructions and transformations of life on the planet.

But with this awareness comes a great risk of renewing the illusion of a 'real' freedom – one more 'natural' and more 'human'. This risk is great, because we still have not progressed in our very thinking of freedom. The image of self-determination continues to fascinate us, even as the problem is to be found in it.

We are touching here upon what I called the ontological content of the idea of freedom. That is: what is it that constitutes freedom, and consequently what is it that constitutes the essential property of the being supposedly endowed with freedom?

It is remarkable that, over the course of the same history that brought about modern freedom, no philosophy and no theology has attributed freedom to humans as a pure and simple power of self-determination. Quite the contrary. One does not find this even in Locke or Rousseau. Without going into detail about the numerous bodies of thought that come into play, one might say that full and whole self-determination has never been thought except as that of a perfect being named God, or indeed Reason, Spirit, Nature, or else History, but never identified with humans, even if they represented its ideal or its absolute. In a certain way our culture was schizophrenic: on the one hand we had to be free, on the other we knew that we weren't.

This is also why we have not ceased to speak of 'freeing', of 'liberation' or of 'emancipation' – that is, of operations that presuppose an initial absence of freedom. But if it is possible for a child to become a free and responsible adult, if it is possible to definitively liberate a prisoner, and if it is possible to overthrow a tyrant, it is not certain, for all that, that we can, in like manner, cause an absolute subject to come about through its own autonomy.

We have been able to represent such a subject only in three forms, and each of the three ends in a limitation of autonomy – and consequently in a self-limitation.

The first form is that of libertinism, which in its strong and initial sense represents the principle of a complete independence from all manner of laws and codes that are recognized by a society. Libertine autonomy is that of an unmediated wanting or desiring, in all the effervescence that it can offer. The undeniable seductiveness of its image cannot prevent this effervescence from getting carried away and destroying itself – which is not a matter of exhaustion, but rather of implosion through excess. Indeed, what is proper to the libertine is to venture (at the risk of self) outside all being proper.

The second form is the one represented by the association of Kant and Sade such as Lacan expounded it. This is an absolute subject's certainty about its own law – one assigned by Kant to a universal rationality and by Sade to a no less universal subjectivity, the former supposing an absolute dignity, the latter a no less absolute cruelty. This ambivalence ends up in an internal contradiction, indeed a self-expropriation, of freedom.

The third form is given in what Marx calls free labour, that is, the free production of the being who is as much social as individual. This production assumes the definition of a product. Now this is exactly what Marx does not know how to determine other than as free labour itself. In other words, freedom becomes its own production – it is not a property given in advance or a right. It is its own act – but at the same time it in fact presupposes itself, just as much as the full autonomy of an absolute being. In doing so it loses itself, because it either merely reproduces itself or is reduced to being the force of production of new possessions.

At this point, it must be admitted that the autonomy required by freedom seems inevitably and, if I can put it this way, *auto*-matically excluded.

This in itself gives us an indication. What is excluded is for self-determination to be the property of a being. But it is precisely the presupposition of a 'proper' in general that undoubtedly distorts from the start the very position of the problem. If we know what is proper to humans, if I properly know who I am, if a people controls its own [*propre*] origin and nature – then it is certain that freedom is either hobbled from the outset by this property or reduced to a vicious circle: 'I am free to be free.' (A vicious circle that, furthermore, also ensnares a god who affirms himself as all-powerful, that is, as possessing the power to be all-powerful.)

Now we have no more intimate experience than that of an impropriety. Who am I? What is a people? What is a human being? To this triple question, Kant says that there is no response. Which means that the question itself is not to be asked. It is not a question of essence, of proper nature.

What is proper, authentic, original, essential, elementary, pure, never is, because it must always be sought out, extracted, refined, *purified* (we should think of the terrible senses of this word . . .). And in a refinement or a purification we eliminate the other, the non-identical.

The proper is never presupposed, not even as pure free being. It is not a property in the sense of a possession. My freedom does not belong to

56

me: it is rather I who belong to the free invention of a proper that is always to come, always to be activated and felt as long as I live. My death does not complete it: it shows that this proper is always other and, if one can put it this way, always *ultra* [*toujours* outre]. Just as marine has its ultramarine, and ultrasounds belong to the register of sound, our narrow ordinary properties, our goods and our rights are tied to the ultra-proper of that which, of the one who, is always beyond us.

This is why freedom has no property like that of a right that I would have at my disposal, and no simple identity. 'My freedom', 'a free people', 'free content': none of this exists except as mixed in with everything that freedom seeks to remain unaware of, with everything that repels and constrains freedom – necessities, limits and the weight of bodies, of the spirit, of affects, of relations and of drives.

As Derrida writes, '[f]reedom allies and exchanges itself with that which restrains it, with everything it receives from a buried origin, with the gravity which situates its centre and its site.'[2]

2 Jacques Derrida, *Writing and Difference*, trans. Alan Bass. London: Routledge, 2001, p. 80.

8

The Useful and the Useless

An interesting phenomenon: I have been asked whether philosophy is blocked by the virus. I understand what provokes the question: the expectation that thought can provide a way out of the crisis. That in itself is nothing new, but it becomes amusing in a situation where it is very clear that a set of technical and practical measures is going to resolve the problem.

Philosophy has never been an art of wisdom – even if the exercise of thinking can always communicate some encouragements not to get frustrated with the real, whether with the hardships of life or the aporias of death. But philosophy is above all the recognition that the real escapes any grasp – or, more precisely, it is the recognition of the fact that there can be no knowledge or recognition of this escape and that at the same time it is to this escape, and through it, that we are truly destined, I would say constituted, as humans and speaking animals. This destination is not a destiny in the fatalist sense of the word but a sending, a launching or a pushing. Nothing to search for, neither behind nor before this sending. The human being is the venturing animal, the risky animal.

Derrida spoke of 'destinerrance': a destination to wander. To wander is not to get lost – which would presume that one has left the established paths. It is not to take a wrong road; it is to traverse a space without roads or landmarks. Neither those of a belief, nor those of a learned experience. On the contrary, it is the experience of being delivered over, not only to the unknown but to the unknowable.

From the beginning, philosophy resides in this *sending* headlong. The sending enlivens and animates itself, it gets carried away, and sends itself still further. It spins off beyond being, beyond knowledge, beyond God and every beyond. It is called absolute knowledge or eternal return, freedom, existence or 'destinerrance' – it's the same thing, but in the sense of a thing always evading identity and propriety.

At the same time, and from the same impulse, the same culture of the *sending* embarked upon a project of conquest whose prospects also eluded capture, but that generated objects and practical products that were meant to indicate an accomplishment (machines, speeds, logics, systems). The same wandering encountered forces, used them, then produced new forces out of them. We sharpened flint, and then we bent the bow; we later discovered the explosive properties of certain mixtures. We desired mastery, to protect ourselves or to conquer.

But we also wanted mastery for mastery's sake, in the same way in which we wanted the will itself, so we slowly discovered it, doubtless starting with Kant. That is, starting at the moment when the will no longer simply represents the possibility of deciding between possibilities, but itself becomes 'the power *of being, by means of its presentations, [the] cause of the actuality of the objects of these presentations*'.[1] So the power of

1 Immanuel Kant, *Critique of Practical Reason*, trans. Werner S. Pluhar. Cambridge: Hackett Publishing, 2002, p. 14.

realization or *production* explicitly becomes the distinctive sign of the human.

Marx writes (in *Capital*):

> what distinguishes the worst architect from the best of bees is that the architect builds the cell in his mind before he constructs it in wax. At the end of every labour process, a result emerges which had already been conceived by the worker at the beginning, hence already existed ideally. Man not only effects a change of form in the materials of nature; he also realizes his own purpose in those materials. And this is a purpose he is conscious of, it determines the mode of his activity with the rigidity of a law, and he must subordinate his will to it.[2]

If the will subordinates itself in these lines from Marx, it does so with respect to a law that is worked out in 'consciousness'. And submission to a law that one gives oneself is itself freedom, as Rousseau wrote and as Spinoza had specified for God alone. The modern will became the equivalent of the self-production – indeed, self-creation – not only of an abundance of objects, but of the

2 Karl Marx, *Capital: A Critique of Political Economy*, Vol. 1, trans. Ben Fowkes. Harmondsworth: Penguin, 1976, p. 284.

ideational and imaginative power of the subject itself.

Over the past century, philosophy has done a great deal of work on this notion of the 'subject'. Its complexity, its dynamic character, opposed to the stasis of a substance but pushed to the point of losing all foundations, its fragility exposed to the vast interconnection of pre-, para- or post-subjective forces, what has been called on one side the unconscious, on another the masses or the crowd, and on a third myth or structure – all this has contributed to rendering the notion extraordinarily elusive.

More and more it appeared that it was the *project* that served as the supposed 'subject', and that the project – in the way that Bataille thought it – is opposed to a 'sovereignty' that would be the sense of a beyond sense, the sense of an essential incompletion that refuses to submit to what Marx called 'general equivalence' and Bataille 'the homogeneous'. Perhaps 'destinerrance' is asking that it replace the finality, always renewed, of an ultimate destination – a fulfilled society, perfected humanity. The same could also be said of the Deleuzian image of 'lines of flight'. In a parallel way, psychoanalysis with Lacan widened

the gap between a project of social normaliza-
tion and the risk involved in allowing an unlikely
adventure to speak.

*

All that – which, of course, did not give way to
a counterproject (the very idea would be a contradiction) – constituted the spiritual leaven of
a time that sensed the need to find or rediscover
what we might call, very simply, *the share of the
useless.*

The paradox is that during the same period –
over the past fifty years – the model of civilization
that has spread all over the world has incessantly
created new uses. On the one side, technological progress has produced more and more tools
beneficial to its own functioning. On the other
side, the exponential increase in the world's
population and the growth of communications
have made it desirable that everyone should have
access to all this usefulness. But this desire itself
collided, on the one hand, with the monopoliza-
tion of available wealth by the limited number of
those who produce it and, on the other, with the
serious climate, energy and existential disasters
engendered by the fever of useful production.

The result is a world whose project is becoming indecipherable, indeed catastrophic, whose subject is becoming ghostly (a subject of abstract rights or of a crude belief) and whose objects tend to become useless. Unless this entire machine is running just perfectly for its sole use, in a closed loop . . .

*

The viral pandemic – along with everything that surrounds it in terms of new measures, discussions, contradictions, uncertainties – is a kind of magnifying glass for everything that I am recalling here in an abbreviated way. The virus itself might be new, but nothing else is novel about this crisis. The propagation of the virus functions in a manner similar to that of other propagations that, for a long time, we have been describing with the metaphor of 'viral'. The capacities and methods for combatting them strongly reflect the capacities and ideologies of the political and technoscientific powers that implement them. Our strengths and weaknesses are playing their roles.

Something that is new, however, is the fear. We are afraid of a contagion that seems singularly devious, of a sickness that is quite elusive and seems to cause few serious illnesses under the age of sixty-five (which complicates protection strategies) but which, for all that, threatens in an endemic way, in often asymptomatic forms, and so on. Up until now, such fear was usually limited to the fields of better known diseases, criminal opportunities or deadly attacks. But it was not a diffuse fear, manifested through gestures and temperaments that immediately feed more anxiety. For example, medical masks are a sign of protection and, at the same time, a cause for concern. It is as if a surgical mask wearer could also be a schemer or a bandit.

This fear has something infantile about it. What is infantile is impulsive and doesn't quite know how to express itself. In fact, we are afraid of ourselves, of the entirely unknown, of all the indeterminacy that surrounds us. We completely forget how much ancient societies knew of fear, with all manner of insecurities regarding climate, illness, food shortages and civil unrest. Fear has other names too: horror, dread, awe in the face of terrible dangers (real or imaginary), anxiety, alarm, shuddering at the thought of nearby hazards, worry, apprehension, distress over ongoing threats linked to powers and forces.

The model of 'fearless bravery' was as important as it was only because everyone lived in fear. All life doubtless involves the fear of being killed or, in a more complex way, of killing oneself. Philosophy is not exempt from fear: it is shaped by the fear of not having certainty. But it turns this fear into astonishment or deep perplexity. In fact all philosophy comes from the fear of death. And this fear itself comes from the absence of religious guarantees. And this absence is constitutive of our societies. But that means that we must know ourselves and think ourselves as exposed to death, that is, to the incompletion of sense.

But when a crop grows, when a child grows, when a relationship is formed – social, friendly, romantic – what is completed? Nothing? Nothing is ever in a final end state – or else it is the interruption of a life. However, this is beautiful – as long as it doesn't involve a murder. This is beautiful because, in one way or another, life is in harmony with itself. It is suspended at the edge of its fear. It is lost; it is true, and the others are inconsolable. It gives its regards and says 'adieu'.

In fact we do have the sense of this essential incompletion of sense. We understand very well that life is not about maintaining inertia but about risking an existence. However, what we cannot support is that promises of comfort, assurances of mastery, knowledge and high-precision powers develop a humanity enslaved to a power that is reserved for some and harmful for the greatest number. A humanity deprived of spirit, deprived of the sense that it nonetheless still bears within itself: the sense of an existence exposed to itself, to its own chance and to its death – but not exploited by a bunch of calculating machines. For these machines claim to calculate our lives, while we know our existences to be incalculable.

We must be able to say, along with Conrad Aiken:

> And here have seen the catalogue of things –
> all in the maelstrom of the limbo caught,
> and whirled concentric to the funnel's end,
> sans number, and sans meaning, and sans purpose;
> save that lack of purpose bears a name
> the lack of meaning has a heart-beat, and
> the lack of number wears a cloak of stars.[3]

---

3 Conrad Aiken, 'The coming forth by day of Osiris Jones: Stage directions', in his *Selected Poems*, ed. Harold Bloom. Oxford: Oxford University Press, 2003, p. 79.

9

Still All Too Human

Is it possible to take stock [*faire le point*]? Not to put a full stop [*mettre un point final*], of course, but just to point out some of the landmarks on our navigation through the viral ocean? It has also become an ocean of talk; the logorrhoea that accompanies all epidemics has not failed to sweep us away, too. There is too much of it, it spins, it vibrates, to the point that the word 'philosophy' resembles the tendrils of the vine or the coils of a hissing serpent. It's human, all too human – but perhaps we just needed a little of the all too human to understand ourselves a little less poorly.

Is that the case? Has the maelstrom churned up some curious objects worthy of our attention? I think so. Without its being a matter of discoveries, it seems to me that we can point out some signs, some markers for the continuation of our long course.

There would be at least five of them, arranged under the following five headings: experience; self-sufficiency; bioculture; equality; the point.

Experience

We had – are still having – an experience [*une expérience*] – that is, the test of an unprecedented reality. What will have been properly unprecedented about it is the phenomenon of a virtually global and particularly crafty, complex and volatile contagion. Every experience is an experience of uncertainty. Certainty – knowledge that is sure of itself and by means of itself – is the distinctive mark of Cartesian truth. Far from being exclusively French, this certainty structures all our representations of knowledge: scientific, technological, social, political and virtually cultural. It is therefore the entire order of our guarantees and convictions that is being put to the test. For this reason, we really are having an experience: we are being pushed beyond our programming.

This, in itself, is nothing new. Uncertainty has been rampant for decades now: the world has been constantly changing; our stumbling and our disasters have caught us more and more off guard. But, still, all the political, ecological, financial and migration warnings did not generate the force of experience that a tiny parasite did, giving it the virulence of the unheard-of. Most often, we have already heard about what is unheard-of, but we have not perceived or received it. Experience forces us to receive it.

To have an experience is always to be lost. We lose mastery. In one sense, we are never really the subject of our experience. Rather, experience gives rise to a new subject. Another 'we' is in gestation. Either an experience exceeds and overflows or indeed it is not one. It overwhelms its object with its subject. To understand experience, to identify it as such, means to incorporate it into a programme of experimentation, which is something entirely different. Without such a programme, we touch on the incalculable, which is by definition priceless and has value in itself, absolutely.

Self-Sufficiency

To be sure, it is not surprising that our sense of self-sufficiency [*autosuffisance*] has been shaken. That of the individual, of the group, of the state or, indeed, of some international institution – that of scientific or moral authorities. In every way, an interdependence has been revived: that of the contagion as well as that of solidarity, that of maintaining distance as well as that of mutual respect, that of a social cohesion that observes the rules as well as that of an anarchy that presses for the reinvention of everything.

The most serious indication of this destabilization of self-sufficiency lies in the motif of the 'auto-': the automobile could alone function as the very concrete emblem of this motif, with its breakdowns and crises, the difficult question of its transformation and its social role. The auto-, the 'by itself' (again, a great Cartesian motif), the autonomous will, self-consciousness, self-regulation, automation, sovereign autarchy, all mark the projecting corners of the western–global, technological and self-declared democratic fortress.

Today this fortress is both cracking *and* being reconfigured. We had anticipated a total human but instead find ourselves with a multitude that is being totalized by an inhumanity, or at least with grave concerns regarding its capacity to be self-sufficient. Depending on how you are seeing it, it is either too much or not enough: too informed and not informed enough, too numerous and not cohesive enough, too powerful and not capable enough. Too autonomous, above all, and not self-regulated enough.

Self-reliance – what no philosopher, not even Descartes, not even Hegel, ever took for granted and what all thought has questioned, from Nietzsche on – could well be what stumps modernity. An ambiguity circulates, from 'know yourself' (Socrates) to 'cultivate yourself' (Schlegel), which makes us forget that the 'self' is always another. This is why calls for altruism are unproductive: they invoke an exterior or extrinsic other. For it is an intrinsic alterity that constitutes the structure and energy of an identity – whether it be a matter of a person, a people or humanity.

With the 'self-', sufficiency in general is called into question: what can possibly suffice to satisfy or fulfil what is always too much and not enough, what, instead of being satisfied with being, becomes, desires and dies – that is, what lives and exists?

Bioculture

With 'bioculture' I am not referring to the examination of living tissues in a laboratory, but to our culture insofar as the half-signifier 'bio-' flashes there at all times. By giving it the meaning of 'organic life' (rather than its ancient meaning of 'conduct of life'), we have put it at the centre of our preoccupations ever since we undermined the viability of all living beings. The 'bio-' must be preserved, cared for, cultivated; and a great deal of attention has been paid to the threats that a 'biopolitics' directed at it – a term that stigmatized the calculation of conditions necessary for the business profitability of a population. Now the pandemic has shone a light on the public management (either autocratic or libertarian, it does not matter in this regard) of health, and therefore basically of *all the conditions of social and hence individual life*. Biopolitics – an already doubtful concept – went bust, which allows us to see things more clearly.

In one sense, this reversal is only joining an already long-standing movement towards an ideal of health whose asymptote would be – unsurprisingly – an unlimited self-maintenance of human life (which would, in any case, form a contrast with the conditions created for other lives). We can thus ask ourselves if we would henceforth place our expectations for a flourishing democracy in a biologist politics. Would a politics of life and treatment correspond to the 'good life' (*eu zēn*, lit. 'good living') that Aristotle defines as the goal of the city?

We know very well that the answer is 'no': the pandemic shows us that avoiding viruses does not define the good of a life, either individual or collective. Bio- is not *eu zēn*. But if, at the same time, we refuse to be carried away in the spiral of production and consumption, then it is up to us to redefine a 'good life' and this cannot avoid death, illness and, more broadly, the accident and the unforeseeable that (there again) make up an intrinsic part of life. In other words, and as long as our society no longer bears the representation of an 'other life', we must think life beyond the 'bio-'. We must grapple with what Derrida pointed out as the polysemy of the word 'sur-vivre'.

It is, then, also a question of more than politics, at least if we stop abusing this word by making it name a vague totality of sense where we no longer distinguish between governance and existence.

Bios, polis: life and city have become the most impenetrable of our signifiers – and no algorithm will produce new meanings for them. We will have to learn to speak a language other than our broken Greek.

Equality
All of the above leads to this point. All of us, pressed together in an experience where we encounter the limits of our autonomy and those of our life, we are also being confronted with the equality that certainly we believe to profess but that in reality is constantly being undermined, and violently, in every respect and from all sides. Moreover, reactions to issues of freedom – our little freedoms to move around – have been much livelier, in developed countries, than reactions to reports on inequalities, particularly those concerning matters of health and social protection. The concept proposed by Balibar of 'equaliberty' has never been drawn upon.

Yet we know all too well that inequality has never been so glaring. That is, never as flagrant and never as intolerable. For inequalities used to be integrated into social hierarchies, but these were not superseded – on the contrary – by techno-financial indicators, be they real, symbolic or imaginary.

In principle, our civilization establishes an equality that it assumes to be based on the equal value (or dignity) of human lives (here I shall leave aside the question, certainly necessary, of other lives). In short, it is life itself that automatically confers equality. 'All men are born and remain free and equal', says the Declaration of 1789. The verb 'are born' there carries a considerable burden. Is 'to be born' an act, a biological operation? And if not, what are its stakes? I will not dwell on it any longer – but without failing to note that the same questions arise regarding 'to die'.

Today one thing is becoming clear: we don't know what makes us equal. That is why most of the time we just assume it to be the case, or we project it onto a 'better world'. But real inequality demands of us that we no longer delay a response. What no longer exactly corresponds to the schema of class struggle is nonetheless being propelled by an equally powerful pressure: there is no reason at all for there to be any 'wretched of life' (and, thus, any lives of the wretched), if our *raison d'être* is to be born and die, not to acquire goods, powers and knowledges. Or indeed if our reason for living can only be found in the 'without reason' of a 'more than living' comparable to that of Angelus Silesius' rose: 'The rose is without why. It blooms simply because it blooms. It pays no attention to itself, nor does it ask whether anyone sees it.'[1]

Is this itself not very human? All too human? But who can give the measure of being born and dying, of appearing and disappearing?

The Point

I want to keep it brief; it's just a question of taking stock [*faire le point*]. In fact it is a point without dimension. Just a tipping point, a point of reversal or revolution.

Can we make the 'without why' into a measure of civilization? If we cannot, it is not at all certain that we will go much further on our already precarious trajectory. All else is viral unrest.

Would we be all too human to dispense with the 'why'? But is this not basically what we already

1 Angelus Silesius, 'Cherubinischer Wandersmann', in his *Sämtliche Poetische Werke*, vol. 1. Munich: Carl Hanser Verlag, 1949, p. 289. SC's translation.

understand, obscurely, confusedly, in living our lives every day? We know without knowing, spontaneously, that 'without reason' is stronger and more intense than any reason. Like the radiance of a flower, like a smile or a song.

Appendix 1

Interview with Nicolas Dutent

NICOLAS DUTENT   Touch is one of your many philosophical objects – which include community, democracy, religion, hearing and sense. How do you respond, as a philosopher, to this period in which, even if it is still thinkable, touching has become almost impossible? Doesn't this deprivation leave us, in part, in a state of numbness?

JEAN-LUC NANCY   I wouldn't say so. First, if in one respect we feel numb, we have also been stimulated, awakened, alerted and mobilized in many other respects. In any case, what is lacking is not touching, since what is taking place, on the contrary, is a properly viral proliferation of contacts, messages, calls, suggestions, inventions . . . From my neighbours across the hall to my friends or to strangers in the furthest-flung countries, this proliferation is teeming . . . or is writhing, like in a hive.

Certainly there is deprivation but, like always, deprivation brings to light the features of that of which we are deprived. We can't touch one another, which means that we touch this separation all the more and all the better.

ND   The body, as you outline in various works, is where we 'lose our footing'. Should these 'places of existence', which you also call 'open spaces',[1] experience the lockdown as a chance or as a threat?

JLN   I'll follow up on my previous response: separation is never only what we touch, but that by way of which we touch. Touching entails minimal distance, not the abolition of distance. Worrying about the lockdown is of course a nat-

1 Tr.: The three quotations here are from Nancy's book *Corpus*, trans. Richard A. Rand. New York: Fordham University Press, 2008, pp. 13 and 15.

ural reaction, and it is important to look forward to rediscovering contacts and presences. But the presence of someone does not simply mean that this person is less than a metre away from me! A presence is given essentially in an approach, or in a coming. It is a movement, a being in front of or nearby (a *praesentia*).

But at the same time the lockdown highlights social differences. If you live on an estate where several thousand people have only one supermarket for their groceries, movements and purchases are much more onerous and difficult than if you have a minimarket and a neighbourhood grocery store, not to mention a bakery on the next corner. If you are a child of six or an adolescent of fifteen in a spacious apartment, you are far from the situation of a young person in social housing. Depending on your neighbourhood, your school, the training of your teachers, and the technology you have in your home, you will have well-organized distance learning or you will have nothing at all. And there are many more examples.

This is all a way of saying that the pandemic reproduces social, economic and national divisions and cleavages. The lockdown – to remain with this theme – does not have the same meaning if it comes about in a population already used to living in the privacy of family homes, or in another population, which is used to living mostly outside, in the street, the market or the square, at the café, in groups . . .

ND   In *Marquage manquant*[2] most notably, you give presence to something that has been absent from philosophy: skin. What does the skin, our first contact with the world, say about us?

JLN   This isn't the moment to take up the analyses that are done of situations in which our skins are exposed to being touched by other skins – which is one of their roles. I have just published a book called *The Fragile Skin of the World*[3] precisely because the world has no skin – it is not an organic entity – but its skin is made up of the relations between all of our skins. Of all of their distances, proximities, contacts, wounds or caresses.

2 Tr.: Nancy, Jean-Luc and Nicolas Dutent, *Marquage manquant*. Saint-Omer, France: Les Venterniers, 2017.
3 Tr.: Nancy, Jean-Luc, *The Fragile Skin of the World*, trans. Cory Stockwell. Cambridge: Polity, 2021.

But of course the ban on shaking hands alone speaks volumes about the meaning of this gesture: to shake someone's hand is neither to crush it nor to confront it with a glove. This is already an entire body of thought.

ND   Sleep was also deserted for a long time by philosophy, which held this theme at a distance, confining it to the body's rest or the night of the soul. Why has it caught your attention? Do we need to invent a new relationship with the experience of sleep, which is also the time of the unconscious and of dreams?

JLN   Here as well, I don't think it's the moment to revisit this subject. Our sleep is troubled by the troubles that are everywhere. We are in a time of keeping watch, of vigilance . . . But we need to sleep. I go to bed a little later these days . . .

ND   We are being tested by an accelerated, premature, collective and fearful experience of death and illness. In *The Guermantes Way*, Proust writes: 'But to ask pity of our body is like talking to an octopus, for which our words can have no more meaning than the sound of the sea.'[4] As for philosophy, it asks us to 'learn to die'.[5] But is the West ready to learn a lesson like this one?

JLN   Yes, the pandemic is causing a forgotten death to emerge: neither that of known illnesses, nor that of accidents, nor that of attacks. It is a death that prowls around everywhere, defying all attempts to protect against it. We are very far from situations of war or permanent insurgency, of famine, of nuclear or other disasters, but we have in effect come close to an obsession with and indeed a haunting by death that we had not been used to for a long time. And yet it had already come close to us through various viral invasions – AIDS in particular, but also animal epidemics. Broadly speaking, one could say that, if death had at one time seemed remote, it has now returned to the fore, as witnessed by the grotesque excitement we see around dreams of a life indefinitely extended.

4 Tr.: Proust, Marcel, *The Guermantes Way*, trans. Mark Treharne. New York: Penguin, 2002, p. 292.

5 Tr.: The reference here is to Montaigne's essay 'To philosophize is to learn to die'.

ND   How are you experiencing, or enriching your experience of, the lockdown?

JLN   I have nothing special to say about this. It doesn't change my life a great deal, because my age and my physical condition suffice to contain me, indeed to confine me. Fortunately, the woman with whom I share my life is able to shop. By contrast, the informatics virus – of which you are an agent, dear friend – has come to occupy a lot of space. I'm afraid that it will make us talk too much!

ND   But perhaps this is a good thing, because it forces us to be cautious as well. We have already heard everything about the virus and the pandemic – everything that our software or our algorithms, our lessons, Bibles or Vedas have filled our heads with. This sometimes reaches the level of caricature. Here we denounce a conspiracy, there we point the finger at globalization; in one place we're accused of being cowardly in the face of death, in another it is claimed that humanism needs to make a comeback; here we say that capitalism is on the point of bursting, there that it will feast on the situation. Here a

government is denounced, there the irrespon-
sibility of one group or another. Biopolitics or
geopolitics, viropolitics, coronapolitics ... at
least we will have exhausted the already scanty
resources of this unfortunate concept.

JLN   Not to mention – last but not least – the
estimates, calculations, prognostics and conjec-
tures about the future of the pandemic. Because
this is what is most essential: how and to what
point will it spread; to what point will it have
effects, and what will these effects be? ... In
fact we are less able than ever to foresee what
the period that we are undoubtedly just entering
will bring. This is undoubtedly what is most
striking for populations that are used to a rela-
tive continuity, one that more or less sticks to a
plan.

The local lockdown is minor when compared
to the temporal lockdown: the future has now
clearly become uncertain and obscure. We had
forgotten that this is its essence.

ND   Illness is no longer what it too often is:
individual suffering, a private experience. What
happens when illness concerns everyone, the

entire community: does it immediately become a political fact?

JLN   I would prefer to say 'social', because the word 'political' is used for everything today . . . Illness is and always has been social, I would even say eminently social: it demands the assistance of others, it implicates others in many ways, it affects our abilities, our relationships – and it enlists industry, research, administration and so on, especially in the context of a hypertechnical culture. It is for this reason that the term 'biopolitics', which is used by many to stigmatize and disparage a politics assumed to interfere unduly with our lives, is an empty term. All societies have had to manage, at the very least, aspects of health, of birth rate, of food supply – but of course this all depends on the state of knowledge and on that of ways of life. In the fifteenth century, the state scarcely had to concern itself with the health of peasants, but if there was a famine or an epidemic it had to intervene. In the twentieth century we had to make numerous vaccines obligatory, as without them certain illnesses would have become socioeconomic scourges. There is no 'biopolitics' any more than there is a 'noopolitics' – but every politics has a way of managing health and knowledge . . .

What is decisive is the question of what is expected and possible where health is concerned. When life lasted for an average of fifty years, the expectation was not the same as when it attained seventy-five years . . . When neurosis did not have this name, it was not the object of medical treatment . . . And when we weren't aware of what a molecule was, we couldn't have had a pharmaceutical industry. Each of these examples – and there are a thousand more – opens onto an entire universe of technologies, of economic relations, and of symbolic values . . .

ND Debates around the relationship between the body and technology have been rekindled everywhere. As someone who has had a heart transplant, you experience this relationship in and from the standpoint of your flesh. You recently reaffirmed your disagreements on this subject with the Italian philosopher Giorgio Agamben. What are these disagreements about?

JLN Agamben's axiom in this matter is that we shouldn't worry about health, that it is a petty concern. I agree with him on the condition that we know what to propose in its place. But he has nothing to propose in its place, and neither do I. People have always wanted to live, and always in the conditions available to them. Certainly, if we dangle in front of them an interminable life that is crammed with enjoyment, we provoke a corresponding desire. In fact, Agamben's position is that of an overturned revolution: since the communist revolution has turned out to be technocapitalist, let us turn away, in spirit, from this entire horrible modern world. What does it mean, then, to 'turn away'? Or, as he says, to 'deactivate' or render 'destitute'? These are words, that is all we can say about them.

What remains certain – indeed, what is staring us in the face – is that we are heading towards an upheaval of civilization. But we cannot have people think that we hold the secret of this upheaval in advance! And for the moment it is legitimate to continue wanting to live. We can also die for a cause: doctors and nurses are doing so as we speak. Their cause is our life . . .

The question of modern heroism has been posed for a long time, since revolutionary heroism ceased to exist, and all that remains is fanatical heroism . . . Undoubtedly, we can no longer think in terms of heroism, and not in terms of 'deactivation' either – any more than we can continue with technocapitalism. But we can at least be vigilant, alert, in other words *al'erta* in old Italian: on our toes.

Appendix 2

From the Future to the Time to Come

The Revolution of the Virus

with Jean-François Bouthors

'Death, if we're not careful, could have the last word', we wrote in the final sentence of *Démocratie ! Hic et Nunc*, published in October 2019, in other words at the end of last year. The pandemic, which we obviously weren't thinking about – we had in mind the ecological crisis brought on by the technological and economic hubris of industrialized societies – overtook us. Taking stock of the many crises that were undermining democracy, we called for a revolution of the spirit. Without one, it did not seem conceivable to break with the logics of calculation and production, in the sense that calculation leads us to depart from what Aristotle envisaged as the quest for the good life – through the thoughtful improvement of what exists – and to seek instead the most unlimited augmentation and growth . . . This blind forging ahead, in all domains of the economy, which has characterized capitalism since its earliest formations and is accompanied by growing inequalities that today are almost intolerable, has clearly endangered the survival of this very humanity, alongside that of biodiversity, on planet Earth.

Nonetheless, our awareness of this danger – with multiple alarms raised by a great many scientists – did not allow us simply to begin adjusting our path, as though it were not possible to imagine, other than in the form of a utopia, a reversal, a transition, an economic and social revolution – even though, as we saw with the 'gilets jaunes', the worsening of the situation in countries that are nonetheless among the richest on the planet carries within it a potential for revolt and for uprising that is more and more difficult to contain.

Stopping the machine in the short term, and even in the medium term, seemed impossible: it was unimaginable. No one could seriously conceive of it, unless they disregarded the complexity of the effects that would result from such a decision. By comparison to the great unknown lying before us – ungraspable, almost inconceivable (except perhaps for the very small minority of scientists who study the ecological trajectory of the planet) – the imperfect, dangerous and potentially catastrophic present seemed preferable to the majority, especially given that, over the past few years, the solutions that had seemed so promising in their early stages have turned out to be problematic, indeed impracticable in the long term (one need only think of biofuels, wind turbines, biomimetics or the energy consumption of digital development). The scope of possibilities for change seemed to shrink constantly, while at the same time we moved closer to the wall of the catastrophe. In this sense, beyond a 'class struggle' that is real but muted and in spite of vague hopes to overturn the 'system', a general absence of any will to commit to the unknown of ecological 'transition' left capitalism the leisure to pursue its path. A postmodern translation of 'the spirit of a world without spirit' that Marx once stigmatized.

And then, out of the blue, a virus brought about what had seemed unimaginable, unreachable: the 'machine', the 'system' so often incriminated but never dismantled, is at a virtual standstill. The threat of death – because it has so suddenly and so terribly approached, because it has revealed itself so close to us, because it no longer suffices for us to hide death, to pretend that we can ward it off – this threat has caused us to privilege survival over the pursuit of our 'capitalist' path, because suddenly the price we must immediately pay to death seems so exorbitant that it conceals from us the future consequences of the planetary suspension of a large part of economic life. We nonetheless sense, already today, that these consequences will be socially, economically, politically and geopolitically enormous, and that they could do more than shake the system: they could initiate its collapse.

It may have seemed, in the early stages of the pandemic, that contemporary democracies were particularly fragile and not very effective in the fight against the virus, while authoritarian regimes and less individualistic societies had better results. Five months after the 'official' start of COVID-19, all regimes, of whatever nature, are threatened by the collapse of the global machine. Interdependency is such that no country, however large and powerful, can escape it on its own. This self-evident fact, however, is yielding once more to the blindness of nationalist egotism. International cooperation and solidarity are lacking, as though every country could remain unscathed by the drama of the others . . . Yet everyone knows that this isn't true.

Indeed, one thing has remained constant, both before and after the onset of the virus: humans choose the near over the far, just as they choose the present over the future. This is a hopeless choice, in the sense that it reveals an impossibility of hoping, in other words of believing in a future that is not the mere renewal of the present and its modes of functioning. It is as though anything not present in our field of vision did not exist, except as a fantasy that we can easily stir up when we need to find guilty parties and scapegoats.

The impossibility of hoping and the temptation to assign guilt largely arise from the deeply challenging experience that the virus is causing us to undergo. While since the middle of the nineteenth century, ignorance has been forced to retreat as a result of an irresistible and continuous acceleration of scientific knowledge in all domains, the virus, the pandemic and their consequences are the blatant and frightening illustration of the limits of the power (one that is nonetheless considerable, unrivalled) that this knowledge confers – even as the progress of technology that results from this knowledge allowed us to believe that the control of our personal and collective destiny was close at hand.

The illusion of the infinite nature of this power continues to resist several findings that are nonetheless deeply disturbing. The first is that of the environmental damage caused by this power that is incapable of self-limitation: pillage and pollution of natural resources, destruction of biodiversity, climate imbalance. The second is the sum of the effects resulting from technological progress, such as an ageing population, spiralling health costs, threats to freedom that stem from artificial intelligence, and the growing consumption of energy resulting from the 'multiplier effects' of our latest technological tools and our ever more intense use of them. Undoubtedly the finding that people are least aware of is the dizzying nature of the questions science asks itself once it realizes that its most sophisticated advances bring it to the edge of an abyssal non-knowledge:[1] the representation of science as the mastery of a single reality evaporates . . .

The virus – owing to its novelty, its contagiousness, the speed of its circulation, the surprises it holds in store for us regarding the ways it acts on organisms, and above all the very strange fact that some of the people it infects are asymptomatic and hence 'masked' carriers of the illness – puts us in a situation of extreme uncertainty. In some way, it has set the possibility of death right under our noses, confronting us with the unthinkable and the unknown par excellence. It is not simply the finitude of existence that is difficult for us to bear; it is the non-knowledge before which we find ourselves. The suspension we forced upon ourselves during the lockdown, to attempt to ward off death and ensure our survival, brought us away from all the paths that calculation had allowed us to lay out for ourselves.

The future – understood as that which we project from the standpoint of present data – is fading away, leaving us before the radical uncertainty of the to-come [*l'à-venir*], which we

1 See Aurélien Barrau, *De la vérité dans les sciences*. Paris: Dunod, 2019.

do not control. 'Government by numbers' – to use Alain Supiot's term[2] – turns out to have been foiled, almost ousted, by the 'return' of death as indelible horizon.

The return of the religious, in fundamentalist, millenarian, hysterical or pietistic forms, over these past few years was undoubtedly the translation of a diffuse preoccupation in the face of a world whose increasing complexity made the future ungraspable to many, especially when this complexity rendered their living conditions less certain and hence more fragile. Against the non-knowledge that was taking shape, this return of the religious opposed belief, in other words a collection of utterances whose aim is to seal up the openings of non-knowledge through responses that are assumed to be indisputable because they are associated with a divine authority placed above all contingency. Everything that comes about is thus placed within the empire of a transcendent will in which we confide.

2 Jurist and specialist in the philosophy of law, among other subjects. [Tr: The reference here is to Alain Supiot's 2015 book *La Gouvernance par les nombres*, published in English as *Governance by Numbers: The Making of a Legal Model of Allegiance*, trans. Saskia Brown. Hart Publishing: Oxford, 2017.]

This doesn't prevent it from coming about. The catastrophe of the pandemic is here, and beliefs can't do anything about it. The unknown aspect of all the disruptions that the virus brings about, in organisms that are not only individual but also social, economic, political and international, compels us in the most radical way not to believe in this or that, but to dare to take the risk of living in a situation of non-knowledge – which means, not giving up thinking and knowing, but doing these things in the awareness that, even if we take charge of our destiny, we can never completely control it, whether individually or collectively. Taking this risk means being receptive to the coming unknown.

When the future goes off the rails, when the projection of the present no longer holds, life can only turn toward the to-come, by giving itself over to the latter's uncertainty. It is no longer a question of belief, but of faith, defined as this acceptance of the uncertainty that posits that life can only give itself over to living – for oneself, for the generations to come that in their turn will have to face the challenge of the radical non-knowledge of death, which cannot be overcome in any way but through the transmission of life, and not by the race to prolong individual existences.

By putting us in this position, the virus opens the possibility of a veritable revolution of the spirit, at the heart of which is posed the question of our capacity to collectively come to terms with the absolute non-mastery of our history. Democracy, with all its limits and imperfections, is in truth the only system that can give a political shape to this radically secular act of faith. It is born from the collapse of all systems of theocratic 'certainties', and from the deadlock in which despotic or tyrannical regimes found themselves. It is an attempt to find a way of entering together – as a people – into the time to come. Not in the sense of being able to produce calculations and projections that would allow us to absorb the unknown or non-knowledge. What it and only it can offer is the sharing out, in equal voice, of the respective weights of finitude and non-knowledge.

Formulated thus, it all seems overwhelming. It need not be, if this democratic sharing out is accompanied, as Athens understood, by the only production whose infinity is bearable, that of sense – through the arts, through thinking, through the spirit, through love . . . such that the awareness of the tragic character of existence leads us to regard one another with empathy, because we are confronting the same uncertainty, the same collapse. Ultimately, it is collapse that gives us our foundation [*Or c'est en définitive l'effondrement qui nous fonde*].

Sources of the Texts

Prologue 'Eccezione virale', *Antinomie*,
27 February 2020

Ch. 1 Jérôme Lèbre, 'Philosopher en temps
d'épidémie', YouTube, 17 March
2020

Ch. 2 'Communovirus', *Libération*,
25 March 2020

Ch. 3 RAI, 6 April 2020

Ch. 4 Jérôme Lèbre, 'Philosopher en temps
d'épidémie', YouTube, 7 April 2020

Ch. 5 Jérôme Lèbre, 'Philosopher en temps
d'épidémie', YouTube, 26 April
2020

Ch. 6 'Du néo-libéralisme au néo-
viralisme', *Libération*, 11 May 2020

Ch. 7   Lecture delivered at the University of
         Padua, 21 May 2020
Ch. 8   Lecture delivered at the University of
         Mexico, 23 May 2020
Ch. 9   Jérôme Lèbre, 'Philosopher en temps
         d'épidémie', YouTube, 8 June 2020
App. 1   Interview with Nicolas Dutent,
         'La pandémie reprodruit les écarts
         et les clivages sociaux', *Marianne*,
         28 March 2020
App. 2   'Seule la démocratie peut nous
         permettre de nous accommoder
         collectivement de la non-maîtrise de
         notre histoire', *Le Monde*, 18 May
         2020